GAME ON!

FORTNITE

PAIGE V. POLINSKY

Checkerboard
Library

An Imprint of Abdo Publishing
abdobooks.com

abdobooks.com

Published by Abdo Publishing, a division of ABDO, PO Box 398166, Minneapolis, Minnesota 55439.
Copyright © 2020 by Abdo Consulting Group, Inc. International copyrights reserved in all countries.
No part of this book may be reproduced in any form without written permission from the publisher.
Checkerboard Library™ is a trademark and logo of Abdo Publishing.

Printed in the United States of America, North Mankato, Minnesota
102019
012020

THIS BOOK CONTAINS
RECYCLED MATERIALS

Design: Aruna Rangarajan, Mighty Media, Inc.
Production: Mighty Media, Inc.
Editor: Megan Borgert-Spaniol
Design Elements: Shutterstock Images
Cover Photograph: BagoGames/Flickr
Interior Photographs: BagoGames/Flickr, pp. 9, 11, 29 (bottom left); Joe Gall/Red Bull Content Pool via AP Images, p. 17; Official GDC/Wikimedia Commons, pp. 7, 28 (bottom); Sergey Galyonkin/Flickr, pp. 20, 21, 23, 25, 29 (bottom right); Shutterstock Images, pp. 5, 27, 29 (top); Whelsko/Flickr, pp. 12, 14, 15, 19, 28 (top)

Library of Congress Control Number: 2019943319

Publisher's Cataloging-in-Publication Data
Names: Polinsky, Paige V., author.
Title: Fortnite / by Paige V. Polinsky
Description: Minneapolis, Minnesota : Abdo Publishing, 2020 | Series: Game on! | Includes online resources and index.
Identifiers: ISBN 9781532191640 (lib. bdg.) | ISBN 9781644942796 (pbk.) | ISBN 9781532178375 (ebook)
Subjects: LCSH: Video games--Juvenile literature. | Fortnite Battle Royale (Game)--Juvenile literature. | Epic Games, Inc.--Juvenile literature. | Imaginary wars and battles--Juvenile literature. | Video games and children--Juvenile literature.
Classification: DDC 794.8--dc23

NOTE TO READERS

Video games that depict shooting or other violent acts should be subject to adult discretion and awareness that exposure to such acts may affect players' perceptions of violence in the real world.

CONTENTS

A Living, Changing World.......................... 4

Epic Origins 6

Save the World.. 8

Battle Royale..10

March Madness..16

Fortnite Fever 18

Captains of Crunch..................................20

Coming Together......................................22

Game Changers 24

The Future of *Fortnite*............................26

Timeline...28

Glossary 30

Online Resources..................................... 31

Index..32

A LIVING, CHANGING WORLD

The most popular video game in the world begins with a flying bus and one hundred fighters wearing **parachutes**. From there, it only gets crazier.

Fortnite is a multiplayer, online shooter video game developed by Epic Games. It features three main play modes. *Battle Royale* is the most popular mode. Players fight one another in this mode, and the last person standing wins. The action-packed battles are fast and fun to watch.

Battle Royale is free. But players can buy Battle Passes for special items and challenges. Players can also buy "V-bucks" to make in-game purchases, such as outfits, backpacks, and pets. Many items are offered for only a short time before they vanish.

Providing opportunities for in-game purchases is called a "games-as-a-service" model. And Epic Games has this model down to a science. In 2018 alone, *Fortnite* earned $2.4 billion

Fortnite has more than 250 million players. If it were a country, it would be the fifth largest in the world!

through in-game purchases. Game developers work nonstop to add new content to the game. Design lead Eric Williamson and his team want *Fortnite* to feel like a living, changing world.

EPIC ORIGINS

In 1991, engineering student Tim Sweeney started a computer consulting company in Maryland. Sweeney's business eventually became a video game company called Epic Games.

In 1998, Epic shook the gaming industry with its Unreal Engine (UE), a platform for building video games. Major developers began using the UE to create their own hit games. Epic received a share of the profits from these games.

At first, Epic focused on **PC** games. But in time, the company set its sights on multiplayer **console** games. In 2006, it released *Gears of War* for Microsoft's Xbox 360. The shooter game was Epic's biggest hit yet. But big changes were on the gaming horizon.

By 2011, the video game *Minecraft* had exploded in popularity. Players loved its nonstop **updates**. Epic noticed and began working on a game that could compete.

The 17th Annual Game Developers Choice Awards honored Tim Sweeney with its Lifetime Achievement Award in 2017.

Epic first introduced *Fortnite* at Spike TV's Video Game Awards in December 2011. *Fortnite* players would collect gear, build defensive structures, and fight off zombies. The crowd was thrilled! But fans had a long wait ahead.

SAVE THE WORLD

To build the best game, Epic needed the best technology. The latest Unreal Engine, UE3, had launched in 2004. Epic began developing a new Unreal Engine, UE4, to bring *Fortnite* to life.

In 2012, Sweeney brought in backup. Chinese gaming company Tencent agreed to help shape *Fortnite*. In exchange, Tencent bought nearly half the company. Meanwhile, key *Fortnite* creators left Epic to work on other projects. These changes slowed *Fortnite*'s development to a crawl.

Excitement over *Fortnite* died down over time. But in 2014, *Fortnite* hit the cover of *Game Informer* magazine. The issue featured 20 pages of details about the game and its developers. The buzz was back!

Alpha testing began a few months later, and the **prototype** was finished that year. In 2015, *Fortnite* entered **beta testing**. Developers used feedback from 50,000 players to finish the game.

"Husks" are the most common monsters that players fight against in *Save the World*.

Fortnite: Save the World (*STW*) finally dropped in July 2017.
It featured bright, colorful **graphics** and smooth gameplay.
Reviews were positive, but the original buzz had grown cold.
A different type of game was stealing the spotlight.

BATTLE ROYALE

Four months before *Save the World*'s release, a shooter game called *PlayerUnknown's Battlegrounds* (*PUBG*) hit the market. Gamers were wild for its battle royale style, in which players fight to survive and be the last one standing. This gave Epic the idea to create its own battle royale game!

In September 2017, Epic launched *Fortnite: Battle Royale* (*BR*) as a 100-player game mode in *STW*. *BR* served classic battle royale features with *Fortnite* twists. Players could build forts and towers for defense.

The game's bright, bouncy style charmed players of all ages. Unlike most shooter games, *Fortnite* featured cartoony characters and silly humor.

BATTLE ROYALE BASICS

+ Players start with basic gear
+ Armor and weapons must be found or earned
+ Shrinking boundary forces players closer together
+ Last player standing wins

Each match in *Battle Royale* lasts about 20 minutes. These quick rounds are convenient for gamers on the go!

In two weeks, *BR* raked in 10 million users. Epic soon made *BR* a distinct offering separate from *STW*. And, it was free to play!

Skins can range from cute to fierce to downright strange! Season 8's banana-themed skin was called "Peely."

The tide was turning, and *Fortnite* had the upper hand. Epic worked around the clock to fix flaws and roll out **updates**.

ONE BIG BATTLE!

On February 4, 2018, a record 3.4 million people played *Battle Royale* at the same time. The flood of players smashed *PUBG*'s record!

In December 2017, Epic unveiled a new reward system. By purchasing a Battle Pass, players could now complete Daily Challenges to earn "experience points" and climb Battle Pass levels. Certain levels unlocked special rewards, like limited-time skins, or costumes. Every few months, Epic would roll out a new themed season and Battle Pass.

Battle Royale Season 2 dropped that December. Players scrambled to work their way through the first ever Battle Pass. Season 2 also introduced "emotes." Emotes were dances and other actions that players could perform to react to one another during matches.

In January 2018, Epic wowed players with a major map update. It featured **biomes** and exciting new areas to explore. The world of *Fortnite* was growing at lightning speed!

LEVEL UP!

Fortnite: Battle Royale

Since its 2017 launch, *Battle Royale* has transformed from a simple shooter game into an entire world!

SEASON 2 2017

MEDIEVAL THEME

+ First major map **update**: new locations; **biomes** introduced

+ Battle Pass features dozens of unlockable outfits, tools, and other rewards

+ Emotes introduced

+ Daily Challenges now available

SEASON 5 2018

TIME-TRAVEL THEME

+ New desert biome

+ New locations: Paradise Palms, Lazy Links, Viking Village

+ First motorized **vehicle** introduced: All Terrain Kart

+ Toys introduced: players can now play with beach balls and other toys in-game

+ **Rifts** teleport players to different map areas

In Season 5, rifts gave players a wild new way to get around the island.

Bonesy the dog is one of three pets *Fortnite* introduced in Season 6.

DARKNESS THEME

+ New locations: Haunted Castle, Corrupted Areas, Corn Fields, Floating Island

+ Shadow Stones let players pass through objects and turn invisible when not moving

+ Pets introduced

+ Players can unlock new music by reaching certain Battle Pass levels

+ Storm **graphics** improved: rain and lightning effects increase as storm grows stronger

PIRATE THEME

+ New locations: Lazy Lagoon, Sunny Steps

+ New obstacle: Lava surfaces

+ Party Assist introduced: players can now help one another complete Battle Pass challenges

+ Volcanic Vents boost players and **vehicles** into the sky

MARCH MADNESS

By March 2018, *Battle Royale* was becoming the most-watched game on the **livestreaming** platform Twitch. Top *BR* **streamers**, like Tyler "Ninja" Blevins, were gaining swarms of viewers.

On March 15, *Fortnite* made history when Ninja streamed himself playing *BR* with rapper Drake. Soon, they teamed up with rapper Travis Scott and NFL player JuJu Smith-Schuster. At one point, the stream hosted more than 635,000 viewers!

Fortnite had become a global sensation. News reports ran stories on the game played by rappers, sports stars, and children alike. Meanwhile, Epic was on a mission to share *BR* with more players. A **mobile** game was in the works.

That March, Epic released an invite-only **beta test** for *Battle Royale: Mobile* (*BRM*). The game became the number one **downloaded** iPhone app in 47 countries in its first 24 hours.

BRM brought the full **console** game to fans on the go. A mobile player could match up against console players from

Ninja earns more than $500,000 each month streaming *Fortnite*. In September 2018, he became the first e-sports player featured on the cover of *ESPN The Magazine*.

the palm of her hand! In just three days, the free app made $1 million through in-game sales.

FORTNITE FEVER

Epic had struck gold. Over April 2018, *Fortnite* made about $1 million a day. However, not everyone was a fan of the game.

Parents worried their kids were spending too much time online. Teachers were upset, too. With the release of *BRM*, students were playing the game in class. Schools complained of internet problems as battling students jammed Wi-Fi networks.

Even sports stars were caught up in *Fortnite*! Some were staying up all night to play. Trainers worried this would affect team performance.

Fortnite fans were hooked. Epic wanted to keep it that way. Developers tracked the community's latest trends. In May, Epic released the game's fourth season. The theme? Superheroes.

Marvel Studios' *Avengers: Infinity War* had just hit theaters, and superheroes were on everyone's mind. Epic's team even worked with Marvel to create a Limited-Time Mode (LTM). Fans could play as the movie's main villain, Thanos!

Avengers: Infinity War directors Joe and Anthony Russo are huge *Fortnite* fans. They suggested the *Fortnite–Avengers* mash-up that lead to the Thanos LTM.

CAPTAINS OF CRUNCH

While many video games take months to release new content, *Fortnite* does so nonstop. Some *Fortnite* designers work as many as 100 hours a week to keep up. Game designers call this overtime work "crunch," and it is common in the industry. The crunch rarely ends for a game like *Fortnite*.

Fortnite designers work together to brainstorm ideas for the game. "We come up with crazy ideas just because they'll be funny," says design lead Eric Williamson. "Then we figure out how to make them work." Those crazy ideas include new costumes, LTMs, and everything in between.

Most importantly, the designers study player feedback. They learn the community's likes, dislikes, and latest jokes. This helps them design a world that always feels new and fun. As Epic's worldwide creative director Donald Mustard says, "It's as fresh as it gets."

FORK KNIFE

Fortnite players liked to call the game "Fork Knife" as a joke. Designers joined the fun by adding a "Fork Knife" food truck to the *Fortnite* map!

Epic Games has studios in countries across the world, including Canada, Germany (*above*), China, and Japan.

COMING TOGETHER

Fortnite had become a favorite pastime for all kinds of gamers. And in May 2018, the video game officially entered the world of competitive **e-sports**.

The first *Battle Royale* tournament took place in June 2018 at the Electronic Entertainment Expo (E3). At this event in Los Angeles, California, celebrities teamed up with pro gamers. Ninja and electronic dance music artist Marshmello won the main event.

Also at E3, Epic introduced the 2019 *Fortnite* World Cup. This global *BR* competition would be open to any of *Fortnite*'s 125 million players!

Epic wanted everyone to be able to play *Fortnite* together, no matter what gaming **console** they were using. At E3, *Fortnite* became

VIRTUAL DANCE PARTY

In February 2019, *Fortnite* threw a live in-game concert! Marshmello performed on a virtual stage, and weapons were turned off for the event. Instead of fighting, players danced and enjoyed the show!

Nearly 2 million viewers watched the E3 *Battle Royale* livestream, making it the most viewed Western e-sports competition in history.

available on the Nintendo Switch **console**. It was **downloaded** more than 2 million times in 24 hours. Three months later, Epic began **beta testing** *Fortnite* for Sony's PlayStation 4. *Fortnite* had become the highest-earning console video game of all time.

GAME CHANGERS

Epic wanted to encourage the growing *Fortnite* community to be creative. In July 2018, Epic introduced its Playground LTM. This mode offered users a full hour to battle, build, and goof off.

Fortnite fans soon had more opportunities to create. In October, Epic launched its Support-A-Creator (SAC) program. Approved content creators would earn $5 for every 10,000 V-Bucks spent by their friends and fans. SAC started as an experiment. But it was such a hit that Epic let it stay for good.

In December, *Fortnite*: *Creative* came out as the Playground experience of players' dreams. Private islands let players place, move, and erase whatever they wished. They could then share their creations as game matches.

Epic loved to see what its fans could do. In March 2019, it launched the LTM Creator Contest. Players created LTMs in *Creative* and submitted their best builds. The winning creation was named an official *Fortnite* LTM!

Players in Cologne, Germany, show their *Fortnite* pride by dressing up for the Gamescom 2017 video game fair.

THE FUTURE OF *FORTNITE*

Epic created *Fortnite* with the right tools at just the right time. It became the world's most popular video game, and its creators show no signs of slowing down. Epic **CEO** Tim Sweeney hopes to use *Fortnite*'s popularity to give back to the game industry.

In March 2019, Sweeney launched Epic MegaGrants. The program offers $100 million for digital content makers of all kinds. It also provides free game development tools. "This is our way of sharing *Fortnite*'s unbelievable success with as many developers as we can," Sweeney says.

Many people are sharing in the game's success. Today's top *Fortnite* **streamers** earn millions of dollars. Major **e-sports** organizations are building *Battle Royale* teams. In April, the first *Fortnite* World Cup opened. Finalists competed in July.

Sweeney believes the colorful shooter game is growing into a new kind of virtual community. "We feel the game industry is

In January 2019, hundreds of gamers faced off in the *Fortnite* Summer Smash at the Australian Open tennis tournament. Its $500,000 prize pool was the largest in Australian e-sports history.

changing in some major ways," he says. For now, *Fortnite* is **parachuting** ahead of the pack!

TIMELINE

1998
Epic Games launches the Unreal Engine.

2012
Chinese gaming company Tencent buys part of Epic Games to help shape *Fortnite*.

1991
Tim Sweeney starts the company that will become Epic Games.

2011
Epic Games introduces *Fortnite* at the Spike Video Game Awards.

2014
Game Informer magazine features *Fortnite* in a cover story. Alpha testing for the video game begins.

2015

Fortnite enters beta testing with 50,000 players.

2018

Battle Royale is released for mobile devices in March. Epic launches *Fortnite: Creative* in December.

2019

The first *Fortnite* World Cup opens in April.

2017

Epic Games releases *Fortnite: Save the World* in July. *Fortnite: Battle Royale* drops in September.

GLOSSARY

alpha test—a product test performed by the maker with the goal of fixing issues before releasing the product to everyday users.

beta test—a product test that takes place after alpha testing and is performed by everyday users of the product.

biome—a large community of plants and animals that live in a particular climate and landscape. Examples of biomes include grassland, desert, and tundra.

CEO—chief executive officer. The person who makes the major decisions for running an organization or business.

console—an electronic system used to play video games.

download—to transfer data from a computer network to a single computer or device.

e-sports—competitive, organized video gaming. *E-sports* stands for "electronic sports."

graphics—images on the screen of a computer, TV, or other device.

livestream—the real-time audio or video transmission of an event over the internet.

mobile—capable of moving or being moved.

parachute—an umbrella-like device used to slow something falling through the air. To parachute is to jump out of an aircraft and use a parachute to fall slowly to the ground.

PC—a personal computer.

prototype—an early model of a product on which future versions can be modeled.

rift—a crack or opening.

stream—to transfer data, such as music or video, in a steady stream so it can be played immediately.

update—a more modern or up-to-date form of something.

vehicle—something used to carry or transport. Cars, trucks, airplanes, and boats are vehicles.

ONLINE RESOURCES

Booklinks
NONFICTION NETWORK
FREE! ONLINE NONFICTION RESOURCES

To learn more about *Fortnite*, please visit **abdobooklinks.com** or scan this QR code. These links are routinely monitored and updated to provide the most current information available.

INDEX

alpha testing, 8
Avengers: Infinity War, 18

Battle Passes, 4, 13, 14, 15
Battle Royale, 4, 10, 11, 13, 14, 15, 16, 18, 22, 26
beta testing, 8, 16, 23
biomes, 13, 14
Blevins, Tyler (Ninja), 16, 22

California, 22
characters, 10, 15, 18
concerns, 18
Creative, 24

developers, 4, 5, 6, 8, 18, 26
downloads, 16, 23
Drake, 16

Electronic Entertainment Expo, 22, 23
emotes, 13, 14
Epic Games, 4, 6, 7, 8, 10, 11, 13, 16, 18, 20, 22, 23, 24, 26
Epic MegaGrants, 26

Fortnite World Cup, 22, 26

game designers, 5, 20, 21
Game Informer, 8
Gears of War, 6
graphics, 9, 15

livestreaming, 16, 26

Marshmello, 22
Marvel Studios, 18
Maryland, 6
Microsoft, 6
Minecraft, 6
mobile app, 16, 17, 18
modes, 4, 10, 18, 20, 24
Mustard, Donald, 20

Nintendo, 23

PlayerUnknown's Battlegrounds, 10, 13
PlayStation, 23
prototype, 8

sales, 4, 5, 17, 18, 23
Save the World, 9, 10, 11
Scott, Travis, 16

skins, 13
Smith-Schuster, JuJu, 16
Sony, 23
Spike TV's Video Game Awards, 7
Support-A-Creator program, 24
Sweeney, Tim, 6, 8, 26, 27
Switch, 23

Tencent, 8
Twitch, 16

Unreal Engine, 6, 8
updates, 5, 6, 13, 14

V-Bucks, 4, 24

Williamson, Eric, 5, 20

Xbox, 6